T0021414

Ultimate Dad Night

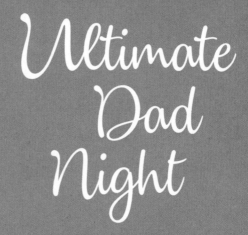

75
AMAZING
ACTIVITIES
FOR DADS
AND KIDS

JAY AND LAURA LAFFOON

BroadStreet
PUBLISHING

BroadStreet Publishing® Group, LLC
Savage, Minnesota, USA
BroadStreetPublishing.com

Ultimate Dad Night: 75 Amazing Activities for Dads and Kids
Copyright © 2023 Jay and Laura Laffoon

9781424564675 (faux)
9781424564682 (ebook)

All rights reserved. No part of this book may be reproduced in any form, except for brief quotations in printed reviews, without permission in writing from the publisher.

Unless indicated otherwise, all Scripture quotations are taken from The Holy Bible, New International Version® NIV®. Copyright © 1973, 1978, 1984, 2011 by Biblica, Inc.™ Used by permission. All rights reserved worldwide. Scripture marked KJV is taken from the King James Version of the Bible, public domain. Scripture quotations marked CEB are taken from the Common English Bible, copyright © 2011 by Common English Bible.

Stock or custom editions of BroadStreet Publishing titles may be purchased in bulk for educational, business, ministry, fundraising, or sales promotional use. For information, please email orders@broadstreetpublishing.com.

Cover and interior by Garborg Design Works | garborgdesign.com

Printed in China

23 24 25 26 27 5 4 3 2 1

Dedication

Dads come in all shapes and sizes.
This book is dedicated to every dad
who loves his kids like our dads loved us.

Contents

Getting Started

This book is designed to make it easy and fun for dads and their kids to spend quality time together. Start by picking an activity to do together and follow the instructions for the activity. Once completed, use the "Closer Together" questions to get the kids talking. As you intentionally listen to your children, this will also enhance the bonding process, which is so important in parent-child relationships. Then, you can smoothly segue into the "Closer to God" section, which includes a Scripture passage, devotion, and prayer. Finish with the "Remember Together" section. Positive childhood and teen memories are a great way to build strong social and emotional bonds with your children. Further, as the kids age out of the house, it will give you a heart full of memories to love.

While some of the activities are seasonal, you can do others at any time of the year, so don't feel you have to walk linearly through the book. Feel free to bounce around.

Blessings,

Jay and Laura

COST

Ⓢ = Little to no cost

Ⓢ Ⓢ = Five to fifteen dollars per child

Ⓢ Ⓢ Ⓢ = More than fifteen dollars per child

Ⓥ Varies = Dependent on how much you want to spend

TIME

⏰ = 0–2 hours

⏰ ⏰ = 2–4 hours

⏰ ⏰ ⏰ = 4–12 hours

⏰ ⏰ ⏰ ⏰ = 12 or more hours (some of these activities may span several days)

ADVENTURE LEVEL

Ⓐ = Low adventure

Ⓐ Ⓐ = Some adventure

Ⓐ Ⓐ Ⓐ = More adventure

Ⓥ Varies = Dependent on your adventure comfort level

AGE

The age listed is the youngest we feel comfortable recommending. Depending on the child, this range may vary.

= 3+

= 5+

= 8+

= 10+

SEASON

While you can do some activities year-round, others are better during a particular time of the year. This may also depend on where you live and whether you prefer to do the activity indoors or outdoors.

Sp Spring

Su Summer

F Fall

W Winter

Rock Climbing

$ $ $ / A A A # # #

ACTIVITY

Find a climbing wall near you. Sometimes sporting goods stores will have them as well as a local college or university, a local recreation center, or a local camp.

CLOSER TOGETHER

Were you mostly scared or excited about climbing the wall? Once you knew the belayer was not going to let you fall, did it make it more fun? What is one area in your life where you need to trust God more?

Closer to God

Now faith is confidence in what we hope for
and assurance about what we do not see.

HEBREWS 11:1

"On belay!" "Belay on!" "Climbing!" "Climb on!" Every experienced rock climber knows these phrases and the importance of trusting your belayer. A belayer literally holds the rope that keeps you from falling if you were to misstep or miss a handhold. Generally speaking, this person is behind you and on the ground. You must have faith in that person's ability to give you enough slack in the line to climb yet remain mindful in case you were to fall. As the verse says, "Now faith is confidence in what we hope for and assurance about what we do not see." We do not see the belayers, but we put our faith in them, trusting that they will do the job of keeping us safe. The same is true with God. While we may not see him, we trust that he is there to keep us safe.

God in heaven, as we trust our belayer when we climb, may we trust in you as we walk through life knowing how much you love us.

Remember Together

Remember, God is the ultimate belayer and will always catch you when you trip or fall.

Bonfire

S J A A # # Su F

ACTIVITY

Paper or fire starter. Kindling. Wood. Depending on where you live, you may or may not need a permit to have a fire. If you live in an area where you cannot have a fire, find a local campground and make your fire there. To add to the fun, roast hot dogs and make s'mores. Take special care to your build your bonfire in such a way that it will only take one match to start the fire. It's recommended that you form a tepee with your kindling. Put paper or another fire starter inside the tepee. Use one match to light it all. Once the kindling is burning, take care when adding wood logs to the fire so you don't snuff it out.

CLOSER TOGETHER

Has something someone said hurt your feelings? Have you said something that hurt someone else's feelings? Can you establish a secret code word like *toothpaste* for when someone says something that might be hurtful?

CLOSER TO GOD

Likewise, the tongue is a small part of the body, but it makes great boasts. Consider what a great forest is set on fire by a small spark.

JAMES 3:5

How many times have we said something that hurt another person? This passage of Scripture makes it clear that while our tongue is a small part of our body, it can burn like fire when we speak unkind words. Often we think our words are not that big of a deal, but we fail to see the other person's perspective. Our words are like toothpaste squeezed from a tube. Once they come out, we cannot put them back in.

Dear God, help us to remember to speak kind words to others, encouraging them.

REMEMBER TOGETHER

Let's remember that words, like a fire, can make us warm or can hurt us.

ACTIVITY

Load everybody up in the car and head to the grocery store for pizza ingredients. Everyone gets to pick out their own toppings. Head back home and begin pizza making. Everyone gets a tortilla. Spread on pizza sauce, cheese, and whatever toppings you choose for your own unique pizza. Bake for ten minutes on a cookie sheet at 350 degrees. As you eat, ask the questions below and read the verse and the devotion.

CLOSER TOGETHER

Why did you choose the toppings you did? Would you choose something different next time? God has put his thumbprint on you; how has he made you unique?

Closer to God

I praise you because I am fearfully and wonderfully made; your works are wonderful, I know that full well.

PSALM 139:14

Facebook, Instagram, TikTok, and all platforms of social media tend to make us feel as if we are not as talented as others. We think we don't measure up as we see what others post on social media. We see the successes they post, not the failures. We see the good, not the bad.

What we need to remember is that people post their A game on social media. It is not real life. God has gifted you with unique gifts and abilities to accomplish something specific for his kingdom. As the verse reads, you have been wonderfully made by God!

Dear God, help us to celebrate each other's differences. Help us to remember that you have made us unique for a reason.

Remember Together

God's thumbprint on us has made us each unique with different gifts and abilities. Let us celebrate those gifts by encouraging each other in our differences.

4

Kite Flying

Ⓢ Ⓢ ❨ Ⓐ Ⓐ # # Sᴘ

ACTIVITY

Springtime is time to go fly a kite! Travel together to a local dollar store, Walmart, grocery store, hardware store, or toy store. Everyone gets to pick out their favorite kite to build and fly. Also, buy some light snacks and soft drinks. After your purchases, head to a local park. Sit at a picnic table and build your kites. Then move out to a field and fly your kites. Be sure to stand far enough away from each other so that lines don't get tangled, and Dad, you serve as a troubleshooter in case there is a kite that is having trouble flying.

CLOSER TOGETHER

Why did you pick your particular kite? Was it easier or harder to fly a kite than you expected? Did you enjoy being outdoors now that spring has come? What is your favorite time of year, and why do you enjoy it?

CLOSER TO GOD

There is a time for everything,
and a season for every activity under the heavens.
ECCLESIASTES 3:1

Spring is an amazing time of year. Everything is coming to life! The days are getting longer, and the grass becomes greener. Flowers start to push their way out of the soil, and trees bloom with beautiful buds. Spring is an excellent time to "renew" our life with God. Sometimes we can get cold and dreary like a winter day when it comes to loving God and following his ways. While God remains the same during every season, we tend to vary in our outlook on him.

God in heaven, we know your love is constant. May we take this time to renew our love for you.

REMEMBER TOGETHER

Spring is a time when the earth comes to life after a long winter. Let's continually renew our love for God in each season of the year.

5

Outdoor Movie Night

Ⓢ Ⓢ 🄹 🄹 Ⓐ Ⓐ # S u

ACTIVITY

Rent or purchase an outdoor movie projector and screen. Or, if you have a big enough TV, purchase a fifty-foot cable. Either way, involve the kids and set up an outdoor theater in your backyard. Along with the projector and screen, bring out the camp chairs, some blankets, or beanbag chairs. Now that your theater is set up, head inside, pop some popcorn, and pour some soft drinks for everyone to enjoy. Stream one or two movies that will appeal to all the kids and enjoy a fun outdoor movie night. When the movies are over, turn out all the lights, lie on your backs on the blankets, and stare up at the stars.

CLOSER TOGETHER

Which was your favorite movie tonight? Why? Did you ever think you'd put together a movie theater in your backyard? As you looked at the stars, what came to mind? Is it hard to imagine that God spoke and the stars fell into place?

CLOSER TO GOD

He took [Abram] outside and said, "Look up at the sky and count the stars—if indeed you can count them."

GENESIS 15:5

God instructed Abram to look to the night sky and attempt to count the stars. Impossible! Yet, God placed every star in its place and even named each and every star. It's one of the dazzling displays of God's might and power and the vast creation he has made for us to enjoy. Stars are just one way God's creation shows us his power and majesty.

God in heaven, as we gaze at the stars above, may we remember your power and majesty. May we also remember that the God who placed the stars in the sky loves us unconditionally.

REMEMBER TOGETHER

The God who made the heavens loves us!

Budget Battle

ACTIVITY

Go to your local thrift store and give everyone five dollars to spend on one item. Have them hide the item in their shopping bag until you get home. When you get home, make some light snacks and soft drinks and sit down at the kitchen table. Starting with the youngest, have them reveal what they bought with their five dollars. As everyone reveals their purchase, make sure that all eyes are on the revealer and that each child has an opportunity to shine in their purchase.

CLOSER TOGETHER

Why did you choose the item you purchased? Does it have some special meaning to you? If you could give it away as a gift, whom would you give it to?

CLOSER TO GOD

"His master replied, 'Well done, good and faithful servant! You have been faithful with a few things; I will put you in charge of many things. Come and share your master's happiness!'"
MATTHEW 25:21

Did you know that the Bible speaks about money more than almost anything else? Money is mentioned around one hundred forty times in the Bible. If we include the words *gold*, *silver*, *wealth*, *riches*, *inheritance*, *debt*, *poverty*, and similar words, it turns out that the Bible pays a great deal of attention to financial matters. If God takes money that seriously, then maybe we should too. The goal is not necessarily the accumulation of money but to watch how we handle the money we have.

Dear God, thank you for providing us with everything we need. May we never take your blessings for granted.

REMEMBER TOGETHER

God asks us to be very careful with how we handle money because it is a gift from him.

7

Geocaching

ACTIVITY

According to the official Geocaching website, "Geocaching is a real-world, outdoor treasure hunting game. Players try to locate hidden containers, called geocaches, using GPS-enabled devices and then share their experiences online."[1] You will most likely want to plan to geocache on a day with good weather. In preparation, download the official Geocaching® app on your smartphone. It is available for all devices. Make yourself an account and geocache away. Happy hunting!

If you really enjoy yourselves, there is a whole world of geocaching fun. Those who love to geocache have created terms that you will want to learn if you decide to make it a hobby. For example, *caches* come in different sizes, make sure you sign the _logbook, and_ feel free to exchange *knickknacks*, just to name a

1   "A Guide to Geocaching," Groundspeak, Inc., 2011, https://www.geocaching.com/articles/Brochures/EN/EN_Geocaching_BROCHURE_online_color.pdf.

few. You can also upgrade your free account to premium, which allows you to find more treasures and log your hunting in the app.

CLOSER TOGETHER

What was your favorite find today? Would you go on a real treasure hunt? How did you feel when you found the treasure?

CLOSER TO GOD

For you are a people holy to the LORD your God. The LORD your God has chosen you out of all the peoples on the face of the earth to be his people, his treasured possession.

DEUTERONOMY 7:6

Wouldn't it be cool to find buried treasure? I mean, think about it. Something special is hidden away where nobody else has found it, and *boom*, you are the one who finds it. Well the Bible says that we are like hidden treasure to God. When he finds us waiting for him, *boom*, he gets excited. Why? Because he made us and knows our true value. No matter what the world makes you think about yourself, know that God sees you as treasure.

Dear God, may we always remember how you see us, no matter what those around us say.

REMEMBER TOGETHER

The feeling we get when we find hidden treasure is the way God always feels about us.

Photo Scavenger Hunt

ACTIVITY

Outdoor scavenger hunts are a fun way to get out and explore. Instead of collecting objects, let's collect photos. Prior to the hunt, Dad, you will need to come up with a list of obscure items that the average person wouldn't think to find. For example, a fallen branch that still has leaves on it, an anthill, or a caterpillar. Each person gets a device that can take pictures. Set out snapping photos of the obscure items. Or do it as a group and take turns snapping the pictures. When you are finished, get them developed at an instant photo store or download them on a computer. While eating pizza, look at all the cool items you found.

CLOSER TOGETHER

Which of the pictures did you find most unique? Were there any you thought were "gross"? Why do you think we took pictures of things most people wouldn't think to find?

CLOSER TO GOD

"Suppose one of you has a hundred sheep and loses one of them. Doesn't he leave the ninety-nine in the open country and go after the lost sheep until he finds it?"

LUKE 15:4

Sheep are mean animals and, quite frankly, a little light on brain power. In other words, they are not as smart as a dog or cat. In the Bible, sheep were regarded as important animals. They produce wool and milk and food. So if one goes missing, the Good Shepherd leaves the ninety-nine and goes to look for the one who is lost. The same is true for us. Even when we feel lost and alone, God will come looking for us.

God, thank you for looking after us, especially when we feel lost and alone.

REMEMBER TOGETHER

God loves us so much that he'd look for us even if we were the only one on earth.

Berry or Apple Picking

S ♪ ♪ A A # # Su F

ACTIVITY

U-pick orchards and berry farms are everywhere. Find one close to you and load up the car for some picking fun. Each person gets to fill their own pail with whatever kind of farm produce you find. Whether it's blueberries, strawberries, apples, or pears, be sure to have a plan so the fruit doesn't spoil. Make apple pies to take to friends and family. Freeze the berries so you can enjoy them on pancakes year-round. Oh, and before you finish, make sure to enjoy the fruit you picked that day.

CLOSER TOGETHER

What was your favorite part of the pick? What's your favorite fruit? Did you ever wonder why God invented fruit?

Closer to God

The fruit of the Spirit is love, joy, peace, forbearance, kindness, goodness, faithfulness, gentleness and self-control.

GALATIANS 5:22–23

Did you know that God loves fruit? It's a special kind of fruit but fruit nonetheless. The kind of fruit that God loves is found in the Bible. It's called the fruit of the Spirit. It's the kind of fruit that comes from our heart when we are truly devoted to God and his ways. How do you grow that kind of fruit? By reading God's Word, praying for God's guidance, and hanging out with others who want to grow that kind of fruit.

God in heaven, may our lives produce the kind of fruit you love.

Remember Together

We love fruit, and so does God. May we continue to have God's kind of fruit come out of our hearts and mouths.

Random Acts of Service

ACTIVITY

Make a list of widows in your church or neighborhood. Let's say there are fourteen of them. Number them one to fourteen in no certain order and have the youngest member of your family pick a number between one and fourteen (or however many widows you have identified). Invite that person over for a home-cooked family meal. In the hour or so before she arrives, start to make supper as a group project. (Everyone gets their hands in the pot!) Over dinner, ask your new friend to tell you all about her life. Where was she born? How did she fall in love? How many kids does she have?

CLOSER TOGETHER

What do you like best about your new friend? Did you enjoy making dinner together? Should we do this with other widows we know?

CLOSER TO GOD

Religion that God our Father accepts as pure and faultless is this: to look after orphans and widows in their distress.

JAMES 1:27

We never know how a simple act of kindness can change someone's day. From raking leaves to making meals, we can show people the love of Jesus through our actions. We (Jay and Laura) will never forget the look on Mrs. Philipon's face that fall when our whole family showed up with rakes in our hands. Earlier, her neighbor Beth had called us and reminded us that Mrs. Philipon's husband had passed away earlier in the year, so Mrs. Philipon had no one to rake her leaves. We combined forces with a couple of other families that were in our small group at the time, and we all raked leaves together. Afterward, we talked about how we should care for the widows and orphans that we know and maybe even some we don't know.

Heavenly Father, may we be blessed and able to help others in their time of need.

REMEMBER TOGETHER

Memories remind us that, in life, more is "caught than taught." Remember that life is the accumulation of memories.

Hotel Pajama and Swim Party

$ $ $ / / / / A A #

ACTIVITY

Dad, you will need to book a hotel room. Make sure it has a nice pool. On the day of the reservation, everybody (including Dad) needs to put on their pj's over their swimsuit. Make note of the looks you get for wearing pj's around the hotel. Once in your room, take off your pj's to reveal your swimsuit. Now everyone can tackle the swimming pool for as long as Dad says. Head back to the room for some delivered pizza and soft drinks. Swimming pools + pizzas = great rest!

CLOSER TOGETHER

What were some of the looks you recall getting as you walked into the hotel? Could you have stayed in the water all night? Did you get the best sleep? God intends for us to rest. How can we build in activities that help us rest?

CLOSER TO GOD

"Come to me, all you who are weary and burdened,
and I will give you rest."
MATTHEW 11:28

Even God took a rest. That's right. After creating for six days, he declared the seventh day would be a day of rest. We all need time away and a good rest. Doing something different from our normal routine allows our minds to rest. Falling asleep exhausted after a good swim is a great way to let your muscles replenish. Good rest can come in many forms.

Dear God, may we get our much-needed rest so we might bless others because we are rested.

REMEMBER TOGETHER

Good rest is important for all of us. Let's build in specific days of rest into our week.

Nerf Fun

ACTIVITY

Go to the store and buy a Nerf toy for everyone. You can make them all the same or let each child pick out their own (within budget). Play inside or outside, depending on weather conditions. If you do play outside, make some boundaries so the older children can't run away from the younger ones. Divide into teams and play tag with the Nerf projectiles...Don't worry, Mom; nobody is going to lose an eye! Change teams up and play all afternoon.

CLOSER TOGETHER

Did you enjoy playing this form of tag? What were the fairest teams? Why? Why do you think it's important to play together? Can you all come back together and do this again in twenty years?

CLOSER TO GOD

He said: "Truly I tell you, unless you change and become like little
children, you will never enter the kingdom of heaven."

MATTHEW 18:3

We all know that playtime is really learning time for little children.
Why is that not true for teenagers and adults too? The benefits
of play for little children are many. Coordination, muscle and
balance development, cognitive and problem-solving skills…the
list goes on. Even the Bible tells us all that we must "change and
become like little children" not just in the area of play but also in
the area of wonder and awe at what the world has to offer.

Father in heaven, may we always have the wonder and
playfulness of a little child.

REMEMBER TOGETHER

Laugh and run and play like little children. God commands it!

13

Bowling Bonanza

S S / A #

ACTIVITY

Load up the car and head to your local bowling alley. First stop is the snack bar, where everyone gets a soft drink. (No snacks yet; you need to keep the bowling balls clean.) Next get your bowling shoes, and yes, they have them for even the tiniest of feet. Set up the electronic scorecard and take turns knocking down the pins. For those too little to hold a bowling ball, most alleys have ramps that Dad can place the ball on top of while the little one rolls it off. See the marks on the alley in front of you? Those are there to help you with your aim. Don't take your eyes off the goal: to knock over as many pins as possible. When you're finished, get a snack and talk about the game.

CLOSER TOGETHER

Did you ever think bowling would be such a challenge? Do you know that in bowling, you can roll a perfect game? That means you have to roll a strike twelve times in a row. Do you remember how many strikes you all had combined? Thankfully, Jesus showed us a "perfect life." How could you change to become more like Jesus?

CLOSER TO GOD

My only aim is to finish the race and complete the task the Lord Jesus has given me.
ACTS 20:24

If you aim at nothing, you'll be sure to hit it. Whether it's shooting a free throw, hitting a target with a bow and arrow, or planting that perfect spit wad on your sister's forehead, if you don't aim first, you will never succeed. Thankfully in life we have a perfect target to aim at. His name is Jesus. Jesus lived a perfect life, and he gives us the perfect example of how we should live ours. Read more about Jesus and how he lived in the book of John in the Bible. It's amazing!

God, by the power of your Holy Spirit, we ask you to make us more like Jesus. Amen.

REMEMBER TOGETHER

While no one is perfect, we do have a perfect model in Jesus to strive toward.

14

Disc Golf

ACTIVITY

Everyone needs at least one disc (not to be confused with a Frisbee). Disc golf discs are unique in that they are designed to do different things. Just like in regular golf, there are drivers, midranges, and putters. If possible, get one of each for each child. If you can only afford one disc, choose a midrange. Disc golf courses are springing up all over the world, and most of them are free of charge. Wear good walking shoes and dress for the weather. Enjoy nine or eighteen holes of golf.

CLOSER TOGETHER

What was your favorite hole today? How about your favorite shot? How about your favorite view of God's creation?

CLOSER TO GOD

In the beginning God created the heavens and the earth.
GENESIS 1:1

Nothing draws us closer to God than to be in his creation. There is something special about oceans, mountains, lakes, and disc golf courses. That's right: disc golf is a great way to enjoy God's creation and to realize that he created everything for us to enjoy. When enjoying nature, be sure to remember this is God's gift and to thank him and praise him for the gift of nature.

God of all creation, we thank you and praise you for your amazing handiwork that we see in nature.

REMEMBER TOGETHER

God made the heavens and the earth for us to enjoy. Let's remember to thank him every time we're out of doors.

Adventure to Nowhere

⑤ ♪ ♪ Ⓐ Ⓐ

ACTIVITY

Take a day, get in the car, and go. No map. No GPS. No agenda. Just go. See where the road takes you and explore what is around you. You will be amazed at what you see, and you may discover places you never knew existed.

As you drive, talk about the feeling of being carefree with no agenda. Turn when you want to turn and stop when you want to stop. After a couple of hours, turn on your GPS and head home.

CLOSER TOGETHER

Did you ever feel like you were lost? Did it scare you? What felt the most adventurous to you?

CLOSER TO GOD

They spoke against God and against Moses, and said, "Why have you brought us up out of Egypt to die in the wilderness? There is no bread! There is no water! And we detest this miserable food!"

NUMBERS 21:5

Moses and the Israelites wandered through the wilderness for forty years. You just did it for a few hours. Wandering is fun at first but can be frustrating after a while. Knowing where you're going and how to get there is so much more fun. Thankfully we have God's Word to guide us every day.

Father, may we cast our cares upon you and allow your Holy Spirit to guide us.

REMEMBER TOGETHER

Thankfully we have God's Word to guide and direct us throughout our life.

Museum Mayhem

S S 🌙 🌙 A #

ACTIVITY

The age of the children will determine the type of museum you choose. Younger children would enjoy a children's discovery museum with hands-on activities. Older kids might enjoy a technology or art museum.

Google a museum near you. Make a day of it. Take your time as you wander through the exhibits. Make a note of everything you find that is beautiful or interesting.

CLOSER TOGETHER

What did you find most beautiful or interesting today? Why? What do you find most beautiful or interesting about your family? Why?

CLOSER TO GOD

He has made everything beautiful in its time. He has also set eternity in the human heart; yet no one can fathom what God has done from beginning to end.

ECCLESIASTES 3:11

Throughout history, artists have been creating works that depict God and Jesus. Perhaps the most famous religious art piece of all is Michelangelo's *Creation of Adam*, which is painted on the ceiling of the Sistine Chapel in Italy. The picture shows God breathing life into his creation, Adam.

Father of all creation, you make all things beautiful, and we thank you for the beautiful aspects of our family.

REMEMBER TOGETHER

God makes all things beautiful. Let's continually remind each other what is beautiful about our family.

Birdhouse Building

Ⓢ Ⓢ ⟋ ⟋ Ⓐ #

ACTIVITY

Go to your local hobby store and buy a birdhouse kit for each person. Buy glue and paint pens and maybe even stickers, depending on the age of your children. Set up a table in the basement or garage, and gather around to begin building your unique birdhouses. Dad, you may have to help the little ones. Once the birdhouses are glued and secure, decorate them in your own unique way. Make it special to you! When you are all finished, have each child display his or her work for all to see.

CLOSER TOGETHER

What's your favorite animal? What about a favorite bird? Are you happy to know you are going to provide a new home for a bird family?

CLOSER TO GOD

Are not five sparrows sold for two pennies? Yet not one of them is forgotten by God.

LUKE 12:6

Did you know God loves all his creatures? The verse above shows that he even cares for the smallest of birds. If God cares for birds and fish, how much more does he care for you? God cares so much for you that he sent his only Son, Jesus, to die for our sins.

God in heaven, you watch over the sparrows. Thank you for watching over our family too.

REMEMBER TOGETHER

God's eye is on the sparrow, so we know he's watching over us.

18

Indoor Camping

S))) A #

ACTIVITY

Camping is one thing, but camping indoors? Now that's fun!
Why? Because you can get creative about how you make
your "tent." Maybe you'll gather a bunch of blankets and some
clothespins to hold them together. Or maybe, Dad, you can get
out your big blue tarp and make a huge tent in the whole living
room. No matter the tent you make, the idea is to watch a movie,
eat snacks, and tell stories until you fall asleep on the living room
floor. When you wake up, talk about your "camping trip" over
cereal and milk.

CLOSER TOGETHER

Which did you like better, making the tent or sleeping in it?
Memories are what draw you closer together as brothers and

sisters and with your mom and me, your dad. What was your favorite memory from last night, and how will that help you stay close to us all?

CLOSER TO GOD

One who has unreliable friends soon comes to ruin, but there is a friend who sticks closer than a brother.

PROVERBS 18:24

Brothers and sisters are pretty close. In other words, if someone starts picking on your brother or sister, you will stand up for them, right? Now we're not talking about using violence but calmly letting others know that this is your brother or sister, and they can't treat them poorly. What's amazing is that the Bible tells us there is someone who sticks *closer* than a brother. Who is that? Jesus, of course. He is with us all the time, residing in our hearts and keeping us close to him.

Dear Jesus, may you always stay in our hearts and guide us every step of the way.

REMEMBER TOGETHER

Family is made of memories!

ACTIVITY

Sign up to go camping at your favorite campground. As a special activity, in the weeks leading up to your camping trip, have your kids collect rocks that they find interesting. Dad, you may have to help the little ones. Once at camp, plan a hike into the woods. Make sure to have the kids bring their rocks. When you've found an appropriate place (such as near the hiking path but not on it), begin to build your family cairn! A prayer of blessing on the family given by Dad will signify that, on this spot and at this time, you praised God for his blessing on your family.

CLOSER TOGETHER

Why did you choose the stones you did? Was it cool how your stones kind of went together? If you could ask God to bless our family in one way, what would that be?

CLOSER TO GOD

From there he went on toward the hills east of Bethel and pitched his tent, with Bethel on the west and Ai on the east. There he built an altar to the LORD and called on the name of the LORD.

GENESIS 12:8

If you travel to Mackinac Island in Michigan, you have to rent a bike and ride around the perimeter of the island. It's eight miles, so be prepared for a good hour of riding, but you will see some of the coolest sights. One of those sights is all of the rock cairns that people have built over the years. What is a rock cairn? It's another name for a rock altar, or stones piled in your own particular way to remember something or someone as a tribute. In the Old Testament, the Israelites built stone altars to make sacrifices to the Lord. Because of Jesus, we no longer have to make sacrifices, but we can build rock cairns to make memories with our family.

Lord, thank you for blessing us with family.

REMEMBER TOGETHER

Let us forever remember this day as the day we acknowledged God's blessings on our family.

Bikes and Ice Cream

S S ♪ A # Sp Su F

ACTIVITY

Everyone on their bike with their bike helmets on! You're going to bike to the ice-cream store. (If it's too far to bike, you can certainly pile into the car and travel that way.) Once you arrive, allow each person to order their favorite flavor in a cone or a cup. (Dad, you decide how many scoops.) Most ice-cream parlors have outdoor seating. Move to a picnic table and eat your ice cream. As you do, use the questions below to spark conversation.

CLOSER TOGETHER

Why did you pick the flavor of ice cream you chose? What do you think of the idea of a land flowing with milk and honey? Would you be excited about that? The children of Israel were excited because it was a promise from God. Is there a promise from God that you are excited about?

CLOSER TO GOD

I have come down to rescue them from the hand of the Egyptians and to bring them up out of that land into a good and spacious land, a land flowing with milk and honey.

EXODUS 3:8

In Bible times, milk and honey were treats. They were not necessarily everyday fare. So when God promised Moses that he was going to deliver the Israelites to a land flowing with milk and honey, they were very excited—especially after wandering in the wilderness for forty years. God is faithful, and he did deliver the people of Israel into a land flowing with milk and honey.

Father, thank you that your faithfulness is never ending.

REMEMBER TOGETHER

God will always keep his promises to us.

21

Ninja Training

Ⓢ Ⓢ ⁄ ⁄ Ⓐ Ⓐ Ⓐ # #

ACTIVITY

Build an outdoor obstacle course. This does not have to be elaborate. Be creative and use items in your house or garage. You could do simple things like jumping from spare tire to spare tire. Or tie a rope to a tree limb to form a tree swing and see how far each child can swing. You can always google "obstacle course" and see what you can come up with. If you want to make the elaborate choice, go for it! A visit to a local home store can add to the fun.

CLOSER TOGETHER

What was your favorite obstacle? Your least favorite? Name some obstacles you have in getting closer to God.

CLOSER TO GOD

Everyone who competes in the games goes into strict training. They do it to get a crown that will not last, but we do it to get a crown that will last forever.
1 CORINTHIANS 9:25

The apostle Paul talks about training our hearts like we would train our bodies to be on the *American Ninja Warrior* TV show. Participants spend long hours practicing different obstacles to gain strength, coordination, and stamina. Paul says we should do the same with our hearts for God by spending time in his Word, praying and thinking about God, and spending time with others who are in training too.

Like training to be a ninja, Lord, may we train our hearts to love you.

REMEMBER TOGETHER

Pursuing God is a lifelong training program.

Star Gazing

S) A # Su

ACTIVITY

Climb in the car and get out of the city. Even if you live in a small town, *get out*! Find a remote park, shoreline, or, for that matter, a farmer's empty field (with permission, of course). Be sure to check the weather forecast so you get a clear night. Take blankets and lie on the ground and look at the stars. Have the kids try to count them. Look for shooting stars. Point out constellations like the Big Dipper or Orion's Belt. On your way home, talk about what you saw.

CLOSER TOGETHER

How many stars did you count? Do you think anyone could ever count them all? Do you believe God is big enough to know the names of every one of those stars?

CLOSER TO GOD

He determines the number of the stars and calls them each
by name.

PSALMS 147:4

We need to regularly place ourselves in situations where we acknowledge the majesty of God. Visiting oceans and mountains allows us to see our insignificance and recognize the God of creation and all his glory. Another way to do this is to look at the stars and realize God put them in place and named every one.

Oh God, may we never forget your majesty and splendor.

REMEMBER TOGETHER

If God knows the stars' names, he certainly knows our names.

23

Lego Night

ACTIVITY

Everybody loves Legos, those little plastic pieces that interlock so you can build all kinds of things. They also cause terrible pain if you step on them with a bare foot. The great thing about Legos is that they come in many shapes and sizes for different ages. They are a great activity, especially if your children vary in age. Sit at the kitchen table with Legos galore and have the kids make their own Lego creation. Have them name it and tell everyone the purpose of their creation. Get creative and crazy with your designs.

CLOSER TOGETHER

Did it take you long to think of what to create? Why or why not? Did it come together as easily as you expected? Did you know God knew immediately how to create you?

CLOSER TO GOD

For you created my inmost being; you knit me together in my
mother's womb.

PSALM 139:13

The Bible tells us that God knit us together while we were in our
mother's womb. He literally put every piece together just the way
he wanted. Now some of us might not like the way our hair looks
or the color of our eyes, but remember that God made you just
the way he wanted you so that you could be a son or daughter of
God the Father.

*God, may we always remember that we are your children, a
reflection of you.*

REMEMBER TOGETHER

God knew us before we were born. He created us to glorify him.

Create Dream Bedrooms

$ $ $ ♪ ♪ ♪ ♪ A # #

ACTIVITY

Dad, you can decide on the degree to which you take this activity. Basically, the goal is to teach the kids how to clean their room properly and then reward them with a new decoration or paint job (again, Dad's choice). As you work together, show them the proper way to dust, clean windows, and vacuum. Put on some of their favorite music and make the chores as fun as possible.

CLOSER TOGETHER

Which was your favorite cleaning activity? Your least favorite chore? How can you make cleaning more fun? What do you think a new earth would look like?

CLOSER TO GOD

"See, I will create new heavens and a new earth."

ISAIAH 65:17

In the Bible, we read that God is one day going to create a new heaven and a new earth. The old earth with all its sin will pass away. There will be no pollution, no crumbled buildings, and no road construction. He will make all things fresh and new again. And best of all, we will all have new bodies! No scars or bruises or bumps. And even Dad won't have to worry about his "old baseball injury."

God, we pray for the day when you make all things new again. May it come soon.

REMEMBER TOGETHER

God keeps his promises and will make all things new again.

25

Puzzle Pandemonium

$ $ ⟩ A #

ACTIVITY

Buy a puzzle or two that are age appropriate. Get some snacks and put the puzzles together. If, by chance, one of the puzzles has special meaning (for example, a picture from a family vacation), buy some puzzle glue, glue it together, and get it framed to hang on a wall in your house. Encourage the kids as they find pieces so that they can feel the excitement of finishing a project.

CLOSER TOGETHER

Who do you think invented puzzles? (Many people think John Spilsbury, an engraver and mapmaker, created the first jigsaw puzzle all the way back in 1767.) How did you feel when we completed the puzzle together? What's a puzzle piece in your life you think is still missing?

CLOSER TO GOD

"I am the Alpha and the Omega, the Beginning and the End."
REVELATION 21:6

God made everything in the beginning and knows the end. Why? Because it's *his* story. We are simply actors in the story of God and his creation. We live trusting that God knows the ins and outs of our lives. We live by faith, not sight, because we know the author of our lives: God!

God, please show us where the puzzle pieces of our lives fit together.

REMEMBER TOGETHER

God knows every piece of the puzzle of our lives. We can trust him to show us how they go together.

26

Family Potluck

ACTIVITY

It's potluck time! Invite friends to come to your house for a potluck dinner. Everyone brings a dish to pass around. You can throw an ethnic-themed dinner, like Mexican or Italian food, a theme surrounding an event like the Super Bowl where you'd bring snack food, or—this is the big one—a random potluck where everyone brings their favorite dish and you see what food they really like.

After the guests leave, chat about the night with your kids.

CLOSER TOGETHER

Who made the best-tasting dish? Which was your least favorite? Whom did you have the best conversation with? What was it about?

CLOSER TO GOD

They devoted themselves to the apostles' teaching and to
fellowship, to the breaking of bread and to prayer.

ACTS 2:42

Did you know the phrase "breaking bread together" means to share a meal? In biblical times, they did not slice bread but broke off pieces of bread as they ate. Sharing a meal together is a holy experience. There is something amazing and magical about sharing a meal with others. Breaking bread is so important that it is featured as a predominant moment in Jesus' ministry. He shared his Last Supper with his closest friends.

God in heaven, may we remember that sharing a meal is an
opportunity to share some of ourselves.

REMEMBER TOGETHER

Friends are the family we choose. Celebrate with friends often.

Beach Day

ACTIVITY

Pile in the car and head to the beach. It doesn't have to be the ocean; it can be a lake or even some sandy shores of a river. Take plenty of sunscreen, water, and snacks. Spread out your blankets or unfold your camp chairs and enjoy being a beach bum for a day. Bring along some beach toys to play with and don't forget to make sandcastles while you're there. Ask your kids about the day on the drive home.

CLOSER TOGETHER

Is anybody as tired as I am? Whew, the sunshine sure takes it out of you, doesn't it? What was your favorite part of the day? When we were making sandcastles, could you imagine trying to count every grain of sand? Is it even possible?

CLOSER TO GOD

How precious to me are your thoughts, God! How vast is the sum
of them! Were I to count them, they would outnumber the grains
of sand.

PSALMS 139:17–18

In the animated movie *Toy Story*, Buzz Lightyear's famous saying
is "To infinity and beyond!" What's interesting about infinity is
that none of us can describe it because, in our finite mind, we
can't comprehend infinity. God, however, is infinite. In other
words, he has no beginning or end. Similarly, there is no limit to
his knowledge or thoughts. Only when we reach heaven can we
begin to understand what forever means.

*God in heaven, may we dwell on your thoughts, vast as they
may be.*

REMEMBER TOGETHER

God is infinite, and his thoughts are far beyond our thoughts.

28

Talent Search

ACTIVITY

This activity is geared toward older children who can read from a screen. Rent a karaoke machine and bring it home for the *Family Talent Show*. Take turns singing favorite songs from the karaoke library. (Make sure they are appropriate for your kids.) Vote on who sounded the most like the original artist.

CLOSER TOGETHER

Do you like to sing? Why do you think that is? Some sing better than others. Why? What gifts have you been given (athleticism, intelligence, social skills, etc.)?

CLOSER TO GOD

We have different gifts, according to the grace given to each of us.
ROMANS 12:6

Some people grow up wanting to play in the National Football League, but not everyone has the talent, physique, or temperament to fulfill that dream. God doesn't gift everyone to be a pro football player or even an athlete. He does, however, give everyone gifts that they can use with great joy. God gives each of us gifts to use and enjoy and bring honor to him.

Dear Jesus, thank you for the gifts you have given us. May we treasure them our entire lives.

REMEMBER TOGETHER

We all have gifts God gives us to bring honor to him.

29

Visit an Aquarium

S S S)) A #

ACTIVITY

Get in the car and head to the closest aquarium. Spend your day observing the habits of different sea creatures and watching them interact with each other. Maybe see a seal or dolphin show. And be sure to listen to any aquarium staff as they lecture or give tidbits of information. On the way home, talk about all the fun you had.

CLOSER TOGETHER

What is your favorite and least favorite sea creature? What do you think of a Creator God who can make so many different types of fish?

CLOSER TO GOD

...the fish in the sea, all that swim the paths of the seas. LORD,
our LORD, how majestic is your name in all the earth!

PSALM 8:8–9

Deep-sea fishing can be fun because it takes five minutes or so
of work to get a nice-sized fish on board. However, this hardly
compares to tarpon fishing. Tarpon fishing is a popular sport
because the fish fights back so hard. Many weigh upward of two
hundred pounds! It can take over an hour of hard work to reel in a
tarpon to the side of the boat so the captain can unhook the fish.
(It is illegal to catch and keep tarpon.) Seeing such magnificent
creatures reminds us of the majesty of God, who created the
tarpon.

Oh Lord, our Lord, how majestic is your name in all the earth.

REMEMBER TOGETHER

God, in all his majesty, made us his final and most magnificent
creation.

Drive-In Movie Night

💲 💲 ╱ ╱ Ⓐ #️ #️ #️ Su

ACTIVITY

Drive-in movie theaters are being revitalized all over the world. Most have a night of the weekend for family-oriented movies. Pile in the car and watch a movie on the giant screen. Better yet, if you have a pickup truck, pull in backward and watch the movie from the bed of the truck.

CLOSER TOGETHER

Why do you think it's important to do fun things like go to a drive-in movie? For some people, spending quality time with others is how they show love. Letting your brothers and sisters know you like to spend time with them is just one way to show them that you care. Can you think of other ways to show your siblings you care about them?

CLOSER TO GOD

Both the one who makes people holy and those who are made holy are of the same family. So Jesus is not ashamed to call them brothers and sisters.

HEBREWS 2:11

Sometimes we just have to be family. Family time and family activities show the world we are not ashamed to call one another brothers and sisters. God calls us to love one another, and it begins with those who live in our own home. Why do we love? Because God first loved us.

God, help us to love our brothers and sisters in different ways.

REMEMBER TOGETHER

We are to love as God loves us.

Water Balloon Extravaganza

ACTIVITY

Go to your local toy store and pick up a water balloon–making kit. They are pretty cool these days and can produce multiple water balloons at a time. Fill fifty, one hundred, or two hundred balloons and place them in pails for each person. Then, set some ground rules and begin your extravaganza. See who can get the least amount of water on them and then who gets the most water on them. Be sure to corner Dad and soak him good!

When it's all over, don't forget to take good care and pick up all the busted balloons.

CLOSER TOGETHER

There was a lot of laughing and giggling during the extravaganza. Why do you think that was? What was so funny? Who got Dad with the biggest splash? Do you think God looks down from heaven and smiles when he sees you having this much good, clean fun?

CLOSER TO GOD

"The city streets will be filled with boys and girls playing there."
ZECHARIAH 8:5

Jesus once said, "Let the little children come to me" (Matthew 19:14). He knew little children love to play, and that's why he wanted them near. Play is a gift from God that allows children and adults to de-stress, unwind, and generally promote mental and spiritual health.

God, may we never forget to play in your creation.

REMEMBER TOGETHER

This was so much fun that we need to do it every year.

Night of Lights

ACTIVITY

This is an activity to be done during the holiday season. Load up the car and drive around town looking at Christmas lights. Choose the best light display. Head home and enjoy some hot chocolate and treats. While enjoying your treats, share the symbols of the Christmas tree:

Evergreen tree = Everlasting life

Lights = Host of heaven singing

Ornaments and gifts under the tree = Wise men's gifts of gold, frankincense, and myrrh

Star on top of tree = Star that guided the wise men

CLOSER TOGETHER

Besides the gifts, what's your favorite part of the Christmas season? Is there a Christmas you remember as very special? How can we make this Christmas special together?

CLOSER TO GOD

"Do not be afraid. I bring you good news that will cause great joy for all the people. Today in the town of David a Savior has been born to you; he is the Messiah, the Lord."

LUKE 2:10–11

It's Christmas, and that means the celebration of Jesus' birth! We can celebrate in so many ways, singing Christmas songs, going to special events and church services, but mostly by giving gifts to those we love. We give gifts at Christmas because of the tremendous gift God has given us in the person of his Son, Jesus Christ.

God, may we remember you are the greatest gift giver of all and that when we give gifts, we honor you.

REMEMBER TOGETHER

Talk about the gift that keeps on giving. Jesus can bring us joy throughout the year.

Gingerbread House Making

Ⓢ Ⓢ ◯ Ⓐ # W

ACTIVITY

Another Christmastime activity! Go to your local grocery store or hobby store, and pick up gingerbread house kits. They come with all the necessary pieces and even come with instructions. Bake the gingerbread the day before so it has time to cool. Gather around the kitchen table and have each child build their own gingerbread house. Or buy a large kit and work on it together. Be sure to lick the icing off the spatula when you are finished.

CLOSER TOGETHER

What was the hardest part of building these houses? The easiest? What do you do every day to make sure your life is built on your relationship with Jesus?

CLOSER TO GOD

"Therefore everyone who hears these words of mine
and puts them into practice is like a wise man who
built his house on the rock."

MATTHEW 7:24

The verse above is really referring to the way to build our lives.
What is the foundation of the life we lead? Do we build it on
"sandy" things like money, jobs, or possessions? Or do we build
it on the solid rock of Jesus Christ? When you build your life
around the person of Jesus, you will still have "storms" in your
life, but you will stand strong against those storms.

*Lord Jesus, we praise you because we can weather the storms
with you in our lives.*

REMEMBER TOGETHER

Where we build the foundation of our lives is the most important
decision we make.

34

Wash and Detail the Car

S J A # # Sp Su

ACTIVITY

Gather a garden hose, bucket, soap, window cleaner, vacuum, and anything else you may need to detail Mom's car. Start on the inside, cleaning the windows, dashboard, and other exposed surfaces. Next, vacuum the carpets. Finally, take the hose, fill up the bucket with soapy water, and wash the car from top to bottom. If you have little ones, pick them up and let them help wash the top of the car too. You're all going to get wet, so make it fun! Don't forget to thank the kids for helping to clean Mommy's car.

CLOSER TOGETHER

What part of the car did you like cleaning the most? The least? How did it make you feel when you were all finished cleaning and you saw the smile on Mommy's face?

CLOSER TO GOD

"Now that I, your Lord and Teacher, have washed your feet,
you also should wash one another's feet."

JOHN 13:14

One of the best gifts we can give our children is a strong work
ethic. We can derive much joy from a job well done. Jesus
demonstrated this by the ancient practice of foot washing.
Normally the duty of the lowest household servant, Jesus turned
the tables, and as the "Lord and Teacher," he washed the feet
of his disciples to show them that serving is a big part of their
responsibility in life.

Lord, may we forever be servants to those around us.

REMEMBER TOGETHER

When we serve, we follow the commands of Jesus and get to
bless others.

35

Ice Skating

S S / A A # # W

ACTIVITY

If you live in a northern climate, then finding an ice rink in the winter is not a problem. Often in warmer climates, you can find indoor rinks. Either way, pile in the car and head to the ice rink. Everybody rents some skates and goes to have some fun. You will fall, and ice is hard, but remember, even the best Olympic skaters fall down. So, when you do, shake it off and get back on your skates.

CLOSER TOGETHER

How many times do you think you fell today? How many times did you get back up? What motivated you to keep trying?

CLOSER TO GOD

Two are better than one, because they have a good return for their labor: If either of them falls down, one can help the other up.

ECCLESIASTES 4:9–10

Everyone falls, especially when you are ice skating. The verses above point out how important it is to have someone, or many someones, who will help you when you fall. Falling down isn't always physical. Sometimes we get down mentally or emotionally or spiritually. These are also times when we need someone to help us up. That's why families are so important; we can be there to help each other get up when we fall down.

Father, may we be the kind of people who look to see when others are down and be there to pick them up.

REMEMBER TOGETHER

As a family, we help each other get up when we're down.

36

Zoom Visit

ACTIVITY

FaceTime, Zoom, or Google Hangouts are great ways to stay connected to loved ones who may be far away or just across town. Every grandparent in the world loves to hear from their grandchildren, so give them a call. Make sure everyone gets a chance to talk and even put on a little "show" if you'd like. The bottom line is to honor Grandma and Grandpa by blessing them with your smiles.

CLOSER TOGETHER

What's your favorite thing about Grandma? What about Grandpa? Why do you think they love hearing from you so much?

CLOSER TO GOD

"Honor your father and your mother, so that you may live long in the land the Lord your God is giving you."

EXODUS 20:12

This is the first commandment with a promise. God wants us to honor our parents and our grandparents just like we honor him as our Father in heaven. When we take time to connect with our parents and grandparents, it brings them joy, and you can see it on their faces. And God's promise to you? You will live a long and happy life.

God in heaven, may we honor the generations that have come before us.

REMEMBER TOGETHER

We obey God when we honor our parents and our grandparents.

37

Journal Questions

S J A #

ACTIVITY

Design a notebook (hard copy or digital) with questions to ask family members to create a family history of memories and facts that will never be forgotten. After you have designed the notebook, you can email the questions to your family members and create the book as the email replies come in. Take time to print them out, discussing them with the kids as you receive replies. Or save the replies and discuss them all at once.

CLOSER TOGETHER

What's one new thing you've learned about our family history? What did you find interesting about our family? What do you love about our family?

CLOSER TO GOD

Let love and faithfulness never leave you; bind them around your
neck, write them on the tablet of your heart.

PROVERBS 3:3

What does it look like to let love and faithfulness never leave
you? It takes a decisive effort; it doesn't just happen. That's why
the writer of Proverbs uses a couple of strange ideas…bind them
around your neck? Write them on the tablet of your heart? What
does that mean? It means to think about love and faithfulness all
the time and to treasure those in your heart as well.

Father, may your love and faithfulness be ever present in our
hearts and minds.

REMEMBER TOGETHER

One of the best ways to keep love and faithfulness alive is to stay
close to family.

Local Farmers Market and BBQ

$ $) A # Su

ACTIVITY

Pile in the car and head to your local farmers market. Walk around at first, looking at all the wonderful fruits and vegetables. Then, let each person pick out a fruit or vegetable of their choice. Take them all home and prepare for your own harvest festival. Include the kids in proper preparation of the food as you pull out the grill to barbeque all those tasty vegetables. Throw in a burger if you'd like or keep it meat free, your choice.

CLOSER TOGETHER

Have you seen so many different fruits and vegetables in your life? Why did you choose the one you did? After getting them home and preparing them, which one tasted best?

CLOSER TO GOD

"Celebrate the Festival of Harvest with the firstfruits of the crops you sow in your field."

EXODUS 23:16

The Bible is clear that there are seasons throughout the year. One favorite is the harvest season. All the fruits and vegetables have grown to a point where they will taste delicious. In the Old Testament, they even had a festival to celebrate the harvest. That's right, think about having a party to thank God for all of the wonderful food that he has blessed us with.

Thank you, Lord, for the harvest season and the bounty we are able to enjoy.

REMEMBER TOGETHER

God gives us all good gifts…particularly fruits and vegetables.

39

Stone Painting

ACTIVITY

Have your children gather some smooth stones of various sizes. Sit down at the kitchen table or put up a table in the garage. Buy some good waterproof paint and some brushes of various sizes. Have your kids paint encouragement on the stones like *Smile*, *Laugh*, and *You're smart*. Keep the words or phrases short enough to fit on the stone. Now take the stones and randomly place them around town. People you don't even know will find encouragement from your stones.

CLOSER TOGETHER

How did you feel as you were painting the stones? How about as you were placing them around town? How do you think people will feel when they find the stones?

CLOSER TO GOD

Paul sent for the disciples and, after encouraging them, said
goodbye and set out for Macedonia. He traveled through that
area, speaking many words of encouragement to the people.

ACTS 20:1–2

Did you know the word *encouragement* actually means to "give
courage"? That's right. When we encourage those around us, we
are giving them the courage they need to face whatever troubles
are coming their way. Courage to start a new job or go to a new
school. Courage to battle back from an illness. Courage takes
many forms, and when we encourage one another, we give
people exactly what they need.

Dear Jesus, may we be an encouragement to those around us.

REMEMBER TOGETHER

It's always free to give away encouragement.

40

Board Game Marathon

S ♪ ♪ ♪ A # # #

ACTIVITY

This is different from game night. For this activity, plan out a time when you can keep a game board up for one to two weeks. Buy a board game that takes a long time to finish. Games like Risk, Monopoly, or Catan are good ones. Set it up on a card table in a place where it can stay for many days. Explain to the kids that this is going to be a board game marathon. You are going to set a timer and only play for fifteen to thirty minutes a day until the game is over. Set the timer and watch the fun begin! As soon as the timer goes off, you must stop everything until tomorrow.

CLOSER TOGETHER

What were some of your thoughts when the timer would go off? Can you believe how long that took us? Can you imagine forty years wandering around in the wilderness? What would you do for fun?

He led them out of Egypt and performed wonders and signs in Egypt, at the Red Sea and for forty years in the wilderness.
ACTS 7:36

Forty years in the wilderness is a long time, but in the end, the children of Israel entered the promised land. Sometimes waiting is worth it in the end because there is a "prize" of sorts for your trouble. *Long-suffering* actually means "long and patient endurance." Oftentimes, in the middle of waiting, we learn a lot about ourselves and others as well.

Lord, give us patience and endurance as we grow in you.

Remember Together

Patient endurance is important as we walk through life. It will help us in the tough times.

41

Play Ball

$ $)) A # # Su

ACTIVITY

A great thing to do in summer is watching a baseball game.
In most parts of the country, you can arrive at a minor league
baseball park in less than two hours. Minor league games are
great because you get to see fantastic athletes at drastically
reduced prices when compared to a major league game. The
food and beverages are so much cheaper too. It makes for a
great, inexpensive activity.

CLOSER TOGETHER

What was your favorite play of the game? Can you believe how
fast the pitcher threw the ball? How many hours a day do you
think they practice? Do you think you could work that hard at a
job you love?

CLOSER TO GOD

Therefore, since we are surrounded by such a great cloud of witnesses, let us throw off everything that hinders and the sin that so easily entangles. And let us run with perseverance the race marked out for us.

HEBREWS 12:1

People watch golf on TV and often think, *What a simple game. It looks so easy, so why do they make such a fuss about it?* What is amazing is how hard these professional golfers work on their game. Some spend ten to twelve hours a day honing their skills. Some think they are just talented, and while they are, they also practice with perseverance in order to win at the top level.

Lord, whatever jobs you call us to, may we work hard and persevere.

REMEMBER TOGETHER

God has a "race" marked out for each of us, so we need to run it with perseverance.

42

Prayer Walk

$ / A # #

ACTIVITY

Simply take a walk around the neighborhood, and as you pass each house, each person prays a silent prayer for the people in the house. This is especially important if you know the people in the house; that way you can pray specifically for them. Be sure to stroll leisurely so you have ample time to pray for every house.

CLOSER TOGETHER

How did this activity make you feel? Was there a particular house that stood out to you? Why? Which neighbor would you like to continue praying for?

CLOSER TO GOD

"'Love the Lord your God with all your heart and with all your soul and with all your mind and with all your strength.' The second is this: 'Love your neighbor as yourself.' There is no commandment greater than these."

MARK 12:30–31

Do you know that you can pray to God about anything? That's right, anything and anyone. Today we are going to talk about loving our neighbor as ourselves. It's easy to love ourselves, isn't it? We take care of our bodies and our minds. We get rest, and we play hard. How can we love our neighbor? There are many ways, but today we are going to pray for them.

Lord, may we show love to our neighbors like you love them.

REMEMBER TOGETHER

When we pray, we tap into God's power.

43

Slip Sliding Away

S S) A A # Su

ACTIVITY

Go to a hardware or retail store and get the biggest blue tarp you can find. If you have a hill in your yard, great! If not, find a friend who does and ask if you can use their hill for the afternoon. Secure the tarp to the ground using stakes. Cover the tarp with dishwashing soap and then spray water all over the tarp. You now have the world's largest Slip 'N Slide! Spend the afternoon cooling off by taking turns sliding down the hill. If you are using a friend's hill, be sure to thank them when you are done.

CLOSER TOGETHER

Who was the best slider today? Why? This kind of slipping is fun. What are ways we slip that aren't so fun? Do you tend to ask for forgiveness when you slip?

CLOSER TO GOD

He has preserved our lives and kept our feet from slipping.
PSALM 66:9

Have you ever slipped and fallen in front of others? It's so embarrassing, isn't it? How about saying the wrong thing at the wrong time and embarrassing those around you? Slips happen because we're human. At some point we all slip up, and it can be ugly. The good news is that God calls us his children, and as our Father, he knows we are going to slip from time to time. What we should always remember is that we need to confess to God when we slip. He's ready to forgive us and help us get back on track.

Lord, we confess that we slip up from time to time. Thank you for forgiving us.

REMEMBER TOGETHER

God knows we will slip from time to time. Go to him and ask for forgiveness.

44

Playing with Clay

§ § 🎾 🎾 Ⓐ # #

ACTIVITY

Many cities have stores you can go to in order to learn to make pottery. Sometimes colleges will have special one-night classes to learn how to "turn a wheel." Whichever works best for you, pile in the car and make your way to a pottery class. Each person will make, bake, and paint their own pottery. At the end of the class, display all your pottery for everyone to see.

CLOSER TOGETHER

What did you find easiest when it came to making your pot? What was hardest? Are you proud of your pot? Do you think that's how God feels about us?

CLOSER TO GOD

Yet you, Lord, are our Father. We are the clay, you are the potter;
we are all the work of your hand.

ISAIAH 64:8

Pottery is so fragile. It can easily break. Isn't it interesting that
the Bible talks about us humans as pottery? God knows we can
easily break. That's why he holds us gently in his hands. The
Bible also says that we are the work of his hand. God doesn't
make bad pots. That's right, if we are the work of his hands, then
we are made the way he wants us to be. Don't forget that you are
a pot made in God's image.

*Lord, thank you for making us just the way we are. Help us to
accept those things about ourselves that we may not like.*

REMEMBER TOGETHER

We are God's handiwork, and he made us in his image.

45

Sidewalk Chalk

(S) (/) (A) (#) Sp Su F

ACTIVITY

Go to your local toy store or supermarket, for that matter, and purchase a package of sidewalk chalk. They usually come in plastic totes that make for easy storage. Spend an hour or so on your driveway or sidewalk making beautiful art with your chalk. Draw flowers or animals or a self-portrait. Have each person describe his or her drawing.

CLOSER TOGETHER

Why did you choose to draw your particular drawing? Was there another drawing that caught your eye? What does *beautiful* mean to you?

CLOSER TO GOD

He has made everything beautiful in its time. He has also set
eternity in the human heart; yet no one can fathom what God has
done from beginning to end.

ECCLESIASTES 3:11

It is said that "beauty is in the eye of the beholder." How true.
What's beautiful to one person might not be so for another. For
example, some people think a well-struck golf ball is a thing of
beauty, but others might not think so. In this passage of Scripture,
we read that God made everything beautiful. So if God made it,
then it must be beautiful! And that includes you.

God in heaven, may we see your beauty in all of creation.

REMEMBER TOGETHER

If God made it, it's beautiful—even the duck-billed platypus.

46

Dress-Up Dinner

ACTIVITY

You can do this activity at home or at a nice restaurant, depending on your budget and the maturity of your children. Have everyone put on their best-looking outfit. Hop in the car and head to a fancier restaurant in town. Each one can order off the menu. Or Dad can fix a "swanky" dinner at home with a tablecloth and the "nice" dishes. The kids can help prepare a special meal for Mom. Everyone needs to try to be on their best behavior and mind their manners. Remember, this is a dress-up dinner. Be sure to order dessert!

CLOSER TOGETHER

Did you feel special dressing up for dinner? Why did you order what you ordered? What do you think it's like to give God our "finest"?

CLOSER TO GOD

So you were adorned with gold and silver; your clothes were of fine linen and costly fabric and embroidered cloth.

EZEKIEL 16:13

God certainly accepts us for who we are, and he does not care if we wear jeans, dresses, or shorts. But we are called to give him our finest. What does that mean? We offer God our first, not our last. Here are some examples: A tithe is the first 10 percent of our earnings. People often do devotions first thing in the morning to get their day started by focusing on God. And we attend church on Sunday, the first day of the week. How can you give God your finest?

Lord, may we offer you our first, not what's left over.

REMEMBER TOGETHER

God deserves to get our best of everything.

47

Escape Room

$ $ / / A A # # #

ACTIVITY

Escape rooms are popping up all over the place. Even small towns are putting together storefront escape rooms. Basically, you are locked in a room and given clues as to how to get out within the time limit. It's totally safe, and there is always supervision to help if you can't figure out the clues. Solving the riddles and clues as a group is a fun way to build wonderful memories.

CLOSER TOGETHER

Who was scared when you first got locked in? What was the hardest clue to unravel? How did you feel when we found our way out together?

Closer to God

No temptation has overtaken you except what is common to
mankind. And God is faithful; he will not let you be tempted
beyond what you can bear. But when you are tempted, he will
also provide a way out so that you can endure it.

1 CORINTHIANS 10:13

The Bible tells us that the devil will tempt all of us to do wrong.
Even Jesus was tempted by the devil. But God is faithful and has
promised that when we are tempted, he will provide us with a
way out so that we can honor him.

*Father, thank you for providing a way out of temptation. Help us
look for that way each and every time we're tempted.*

Remember Together

Jesus knows what it's like to be tempted, and he will help us
when we are tempted.

48

Jump Station

ACTIVITY

Trampoline parks are becoming more popular all over the country. They are a great place for kids to expend energy in a safe and fun environment. Pile in the car and travel to your local jump station or jump park. They even have hours set aside exclusively for toddlers. There are games to play and just general fun as you jump, jump, jump.

CLOSER TOGETHER

True confessions, was there a time when you thought you might have jumped too high? God looks down on you when you are having fun, and he smiles and says, "I made that for you." How does that make you feel?

CLOSER TO GOD

The LORD is my strength and my shield; my heart trusts in him, and he helps me. My heart leaps for joy, and with my song I praise him.

PSALM 28:7

Jumping for joy! Isn't it fun to watch little children jump around? Especially when fun music is playing, it's as if they know how to make people smile. When we put our faith and trust in God, it makes our heart jump for joy! There is a peace that "passeth all understanding" (Philippians 4:7 KJV) when we place our lives in God's hands.

Praise you, Lord, for you are our strength and shield.

REMEMBER TOGETHER

Our hearts can jump for joy just like our bodies on a trampoline. Simply place trust in God.

49

Sail Away

$ $ $ / / A A A # # Su

ACTIVITY

Most port cities, whether at sea or near a large lake, will offer sailing charters. Nothing beats the feeling of gliding across the water with the sounds of nature as the only noise. Sailing is a wonderful activity that has a calming effect on the human spirit. While you or your kids might be apprehensive at first, within no time, you'll be fully immersed in the joy that is sailing.

CLOSER TOGETHER

Did you find today's activity intense? Calming? Or both? What will you remember most about today? Can you imagine getting on a boat like this in an attempt to run away from God?

CLOSER TO GOD

Jonah ran away from the Lord and headed for Tarshish. He went down to Joppa, where he found a ship bound for that port. After paying the fare, he went aboard and sailed for Tarshish to flee from the Lord.

JONAH 1:3

God asked Jonah to do something hard. Jonah was afraid and tried to run away from God by getting on a ship and sailing to another land. Throughout our life, God will ask us to do some things that are uncomfortable. We can respond by either running like Jonah or embracing the task and trusting that God will help us do what he's asked us to accomplish. It simply takes trust in him.

Lord, when faced with a tough situation, may we remember you are here to be our guide.

REMEMBER TOGETHER

When God asks us to do something, he will give us everything we need to accomplish the task.

50

I Can. Canoe?

Ⓢ Ⓢ Ⓢ ♪ ♪ ♪ Ⓐ Ⓐ Ⓐ # # # Su

ACTIVITY

Find a local canoe livery and reserve a canoe or two-person kayak, depending on how many kids you have. Pack a picnic lunch in a waterproof bag or cooler, and bring plenty of water to stay hydrated on the river. Take the first few minutes to get comfortable with the canoe and with each other in the vessel. In other words, find your rhythm as you paddle along. Don't be in a hurry. Instead, enjoy the scenery as you float down the waterway.

After a while, start looking for a place to pull off and have your picnic. Get back in the canoe and simply float with the current. Sit silently and listen to nature's sounds.

CLOSER TOGETHER

What was your favorite sound today? Can you imitate it? How can you praise God today?

CLOSER TO GOD

Let everything that has breath praise the LORD. Praise the LORD.
PSALM 150:6

God created everything to bring praise to him. Why? Because he's God. He literally spoke and everything came into existence. The only thing most of us create when we speak is a little hot air. So when you hear birds sing, dogs bark, horses neigh, or pigs grunt, know they are praising the God of creation, and they can remind you to do the same.

Father in heaven, may we be your creation who praises you.

REMEMBER TOGETHER

God made the world and everything in it to bring honor and praise to him.

51

Tend the Garden

ACTIVITY

Small hobby gardens are a fun and easy way to teach your kids life skills and have some fun along the way. Most hardware or big box stores carry premade "elevated" gardens. They are elevated so animals can't get to them, and you can find them in many shapes and sizes. Pick out sizes that fit your porch or patio, and let the kids pick out what veggies they're going to grow. Throughout the growing season, have the kids water and weed the garden. As you go through summer, don't be afraid to prune your plants to help them grow stronger. In the fall, enjoy the harvest and eat the veggies.

Closer Together

It took a long time to grow your food, didn't it? What was your favorite chore in the garden? Least favorite? Did you notice when you pruned the plants that they came back stronger? Is it like that when God prunes us?

Closer to God

He cuts off every branch in me that bears no fruit, while every branch that does bear fruit he prunes so that it will be even more fruitful.

JOHN 15:2

Pruning. It's not fun when it's done to you. This verse is clear that God prunes branches that are not bearing his fruit. Sometimes we fall into bad habits that keep us from honoring God with our life and our actions. God will take those habits and prune them away if we let him. It's not comfortable at first to give up bad habits, but once we do, we realize we're better off for it.

Lord, help us endure when you need to prune something from our lives.

Remember Together

While it may hurt for a little while when God prunes something from our life, it will make us better.

52

Portrait Party

ACTIVITY

Get out some construction paper, paint, or colored markers and create portraits of the other members of your family. Draw names out of a hat to decide who paints who, and be sure to put down some newspaper or a tarp in case you spill some paint. Be sure to emphasize something you like about each person in your portrait. When everyone is finished, show your work and tell each other about your portraits.

CLOSER TOGETHER

Whose was the easiest portrait to create? Why? Whose was hardest for you to create? Why? What do you imagine God was thinking when he painted you?

CLOSER TO GOD

For we are God's handiwork, created in Christ Jesus to do good
works, which God prepared in advance for us to do.

EPHESIANS 2:10

God is a painter. Yep, he painted the stars in the sky, the clouds
in the air, and he even painted you! God's paintbrush is all over
you. Your eyes, nose, mouth, and ears…The Bible says he even
knows the number of hairs on your head. God paints beautiful
things, and one of those things is you.

Thank you, Lord, for painting us just the way we are.

REMEMBER TOGETHER

God's paintings are perfect!

53

Jenga with a Twist

ACTIVITY

Purchase the game Jenga. It's a game where you build a tower with blocks that are identical. Then each person takes a turn pulling out a single block and placing it on top of the tower. This continues until the tower falls down. Now here's the twist. Take a black felt-tip marker and write questions on ten or fifteen of the blocks. When someone pulls one of these blocks out of the tower, they have to answer the question. Use the questions on the Jenga blocks to spark discussion. As a result, it's important to ask open-ended questions. For example, instead of "Did you have a good day?" ask "How was your day?"

CLOSER TOGETHER

What is one thing you learned about a family member? Were you surprised when the tower fell?

CLOSER TO GOD

By faith the walls of Jericho fell, after the army had marched around them for seven days.
HEBREWS 11:30

All Joshua and the army of Israel had to do was trust God and have faith that his plan would work out. They didn't attack. They simply marched around the city for seven days as the Lord instructed, and *boom*, when the priests blew their horns, the walls came down. When we trust the Lord and exercise our faith in him, we will see amazing results.

God in heaven, may we put our faith and trust in you.

REMEMBER TOGETHER

Towers fall, but when you place your trust in God, he will never let you down.

54

Vacation Piggy Bank

Ⓢ Ⓢ Ⓢ 🎵 🎵 🎵 🎵 Ⓐ Ⓐ Ⓐ #

ACTIVITY

Taking a vacation is vital for your family to have the opportunity to relax, recharge, recreate, and rejuvenate. Handling money is one of the most important things to teach your kids. So go out and buy a large piggy bank. Take a felt-tip marker and write the word *vacation* on it. Whether you give your kids an allowance or money for specific chores, teach them the rule of 10/10/10. Whenever they receive money, 10 percent goes to the Lord, 10 percent goes to savings, and 10 percent goes for fun! Have them put their 10 percent for fun in the piggy bank, and that can be their spending money when you venture out for vacation.

CLOSER TOGETHER

What do you think you'll buy with your vacation money? Why do you think it's important to handle money properly? Is it easy or hard for you to follow the 10/10/10 rule?

CLOSER TO GOD

"Whoever can be trusted with very little can also be trusted with much, and whoever is dishonest with very little will also be dishonest with much."

LUKE 16:10

The Bible talks a lot about money. In fact, it's one of the Bible's most talked about subjects. As the verse above shares, we have to learn to be trusted with a little bit of money first, and then God will entrust us with valuable things once we've proven we are trustworthy with the little things.

Lord, teach us to be trustworthy in all ways.

REMEMBER TOGETHER

Trusted with a little, trusted with much.

Family Ts

ACTIVITY

When on vacation or even on a day trip to a resort town, find a T-shirt shop and do one of two things: (1) everyone gets matching shirts that are already made (everyone needs to agree), or (2) have shirts screen printed with your family name or a special symbol that represents your family and indicates that you're part of God's family, like a cross or a dove or a lion.

CLOSER TOGETHER

When you get to heaven, what family member from the Bible, besides Jesus, would you like to talk to? (That's right, people in the Bible, like Moses and David, are part of God's family, and you are too.) What would you ask that person?

CLOSER TO GOD

Now about your love for one another we do not need to write to you, for you yourselves have been taught by God to love each other. And in fact, you do love all of God's family throughout Macedonia. Yet we urge you, brothers and sisters, to do so more and more.

1 THESSALONIANS 4:9–10

Do you know you are commanded to "love your neighbor as yourself" (Mark 12:31)? Sometimes that's easy, and sometimes it's hard, especially when "your neighbor" sleeps in the room next to you and has the same last name as you and drives you crazy half the time. That's right, we are to love our family as much as we love any other neighbor...probably even more.

Jesus, help us love our brothers and sisters even when they drive us crazy!

REMEMBER TOGETHER

God's family stretches around the world and throughout history.

Song and Dance Party

ACTIVITY

Gather together and decide on a song you are going to sing as a family. If you want, buy a karaoke track or simply sing it a cappella. Work out some choreography and cool moves and record your performance as a video on someone's phone. If your family has a YouTube channel, upload the video there and see how many views you get in the first week. Who knows, your video might go viral!

CLOSER TOGETHER

Did you like singing or dancing better? Which was easier for you? Do you think your video can go viral? Why or why not?

CLOSER TO GOD

Make a joyful noise unto the Lord, all ye lands. Serve
the Lord with gladness: come before his presence with singing.
PSALM 100:1–2 KJV

Do you sing well? If not, can you make a joyful noise? Nowhere
in the Bible does it say we have to sing well. In fact, it simply says
"make a joyful noise." So no matter if you can sing well or not,
you can make a joyful noise to the Lord! Maybe it's an instrument
you can play or simply laughing (because everyone can laugh);
just make a joyful noise.

Father, may we praise you with a joyful noise.

REMEMBER TOGETHER

God simply wants us to make a joyful noise for him.

57

Tale of the Taste

Ⓢ Ⓢ ⟋ Ⓐ #

ACTIVITY

A fun (and yummy) activity is to host your own taste testing party. Ever wonder which brand is the best? Make it your mission to find out! It doesn't matter if it's popcorn, pizza, soda, ice cream, or anything else. Let's take cola, for instance. Dad, you can set up a blind taste test so no one knows what brand they are tasting. Try three or four different brands and have everyone secretly write down their favorite. After everyone has tasted them all, reveal which one each person liked best.

CLOSER TOGETHER

Why did you choose the one you picked as your favorite? Was there one that you really didn't like? Why? What's the best thing you've ever tasted?

CLOSER TO GOD

Taste and see that the LORD is good; blessed is the one who
takes refuge in him.

PSALM 34:8

Have you ever thought about experiencing God with all of your
senses? That's right: taste, smell, sight, hearing, and touch. God
created all of our senses so that we could experience him in all
his glory. So the next time you taste something yummy, smell
something delightful, see a beautiful sunset, hear birds singing,
or feel the touch of a great hug, know that is God reaching out to
you so you know he loves you.

God, may we see you in our everyday lives.

REMEMBER TOGETHER

God gave us our senses so we can "taste and see" that he is good.

58

Waffle Bar

ACTIVITY

Everyone loves waffles, and there's nothing more fun than a waffle bar. Whether you like to make your own or prefer toaster waffles, cook them up ahead of time and keep them warm in the oven. Now break out all sorts of toppings for your waffles: syrup, jelly, whipped cream, sprinkles, chocolate chips, fruit, bacon! Each person takes a waffle or two and creates their own version of the perfect waffle.

CLOSER TOGETHER

Why did you make yours the way you did? Why do you think it's special? Is your tummy full?

CLOSER TO GOD

There are different kinds of gifts, but the same Spirit distributes them. There are different kinds of service, but the same Lord.

1 CORINTHIANS 12:4–5

Everyone is different. The good news is that God made us unique with different gifts and abilities. What's super cool about that is that those gifts and abilities all come from the same place: God! That's right, no matter what gifts he's given you, he gave them so you can honor him with those gifts and with the way you use those gifts to serve others.

Father in heaven, help us to use the gifts you've given us to serve others.

REMEMBER TOGETHER

Just like our waffles, we are made with unique gifts and abilities.

Family Time Capsule

ACTIVITY

Creating a family time capsule is a great activity to help you remember and thank God for all he's brought you through, so find a container you can seal or lock. Place the following items in the container: family memories, current events, a description of yourself, a letter to your future self, family recipes, and even a current prices page. Anything goes that will help you remember this particular moment in your life. Now agree on a date and time when you will open it up together.

CLOSER TOGETHER

Why did you choose to put your item in the time capsule? Was there something someone else chose that you thought was cool? Why do you think it's important to remember these types of things?

CLOSER TO GOD

I thank my God every time I remember you. In all my prayers for all of you, I always pray with joy.
PHILIPPIANS 1:3–4

Have you ever heard someone say, "I'll pray for you"? That's a powerful sentence because it means that that person will lift us up before the Lord. When someone asks you to pray for them, what do you do? Some people stop whatever they're doing and say a prayer on that person's behalf. It really doesn't take that long, and it is one of the most important things we can do on this earth.

Father, may we be mindful of those around us whom we need to remember to pray for.

REMEMBER TOGETHER

Each season of life is worth remembering.

Heads Up!

ACTIVITY

Download the Heads Up! app on your phone or tablet. Heads Up! is a fun word-guessing game to play with family. Play Heads Up! and enjoy this hilarious charades game as your favorite humans (your family members) shout clues your way, and you have sixty seconds to guess the answer. The app comes with instructions, and the fast pace of the game will have you laughing and rolling on the floor.

CLOSER TOGETHER

Who was the funniest one to watch guess? Why was it so hard to concentrate when everyone was shouting at you? When the world is shouting at you, how do you stay on guard and alert to what is important?

CLOSER TO GOD

"Heaven and earth will pass away, but my words will never pass away. But about that day or hour no one knows, not even the angels in heaven, nor the Son, but only the Father. Be on guard! Be alert! You do not know when that time will come."

MARK 13:31–33

Jesus tells us that no one knows the time or season when God will return and create a new heaven and a new earth. But he says we are to be on guard and alert. That means we should always live our lives as if everything could change in an instant. When we live that way, we live with anticipation of what wonderful things God will do.

Come, Lord Jesus, come.

REMEMBER TOGETHER

Even when life gets noisy, we need to focus on the Lord.

61

Christmas in July

$ $ $ 🖊 🖊 A A # Su

ACTIVITY

Pick a day near the end of July and load up the car and head to the mall. It's Christmas in July (also known as back-to-school shopping). Get the kids new clothes, shoes, backpacks, and accessories for the new school year. Be sure to set a budget for each. Let the older kids pick out their own clothes and shoes but make them stick to the budget. End your day with a meal at a favorite restaurant to complete this "Christmas in July" celebration.

CLOSER TOGETHER

Why do you think we celebrate "Christmas in July"? Did you know that God is the original creator of celebrations? How can buying new clothes and shoes honor God?

"Speak to the Israelites and say to them: 'These are my appointed festivals, the appointed festivals of the LORD, which you are to proclaim as sacred assemblies.'"

LEVITICUS 23:2

Did you know God loves a good party? The Old Testament is filled with feasts and festivals that God told the children of Israel to celebrate. Too many people think God is an old, boring ruler of the universe, but nothing could be further from the truth. God loves a good party.

God, may we learn to celebrate you!

REMEMBER TOGETHER

God loves a good celebration.

62

Flashlight Tag

ACTIVITY

Everyone gets a flashlight. Create boundaries for your game, like your own yard but not the neighbor's. Divide into teams. The objective is to sneak around the yard in the darkness, and when you see someone from the opposing team, turn on your flashlight and illuminate them! Once you've been illuminated, you have to sit out until the next round. The last player standing wins for their team.

CLOSER TOGETHER

Were you afraid out there in the dark? Why or why not? Did it startle you when someone shined their light on you? In the Bible, we are told to shine our light on others. How can you do that?

CLOSER TO GOD

Light shines on the righteous and joy on the upright in heart.

PSALM 97:11

In the creation story, the first thing God did was say, "Let there be light" (Genesis 1:3). Instantly the sun and the stars began to shine. Isn't it funny that we feel safe when the sun is shining, but put us in pitch-black darkness, and it's a whole different story? Thoughts creep into our heads about what might be lurking in the darkness, even if we are in our own home. God calls us to let our light shine in the darkness of this world.

God, may your light in us shine for the world to see.

REMEMBER TOGETHER

God not only created light, but he also is light, and his light shines through us.

63

Putt-Putt

ACTIVITY

Most people live within twenty minutes of a miniature golf course. Nothing beats playing miniature golf with your family. There's always lots of laughs and lots of fun when someone sinks a hole in one. Pile in the car and head on out to play some Putt-Putt. Dad, be sure to "fit" the kids with the right length putter. Littler kids might want a bigger putter to feel "big," but eventually, that long putter will be a detriment to their fun. Put names in a hat to decide the order of play. Be sure to grab some snacks after the round.

CLOSER TOGETHER

What was your favorite hole? Your least favorite? Did you find that you played better if you concentrated on and really looked at the ball?

CLOSER TO GOD

Therefore I do not run like someone running aimlessly; I do not fight like a boxer beating the air.

1 CORINTHIANS 9:26

If you aim at nothing, you will hit it every time. In most every sport, you have to take aim with your eyes. The Bible talks about having our eyes fixed on Jesus, the author and perfecter of our faith (Hebrews 12:2). The Bible also says that we run with perseverance the race marked out before us, not running aimlessly (v. 1). Whatever our eyes are looking at is what we will move toward, so fix your eyes on Jesus!

Jesus, may we fix our eyes on you each and every day.

REMEMBER TOGETHER

We can place our eyes on Jesus to run our race.

ACTIVITY

Go to the video game store and rent or buy a game no one in the family has ever played. This will even the playing field. With no one having knowledge of the game, create a round-robin tournament where everyone plays everyone once. Then create a bracket and play until you find a winner. Be sure to break out the snacks once the first child has been eliminated so everyone stays involved.

CLOSER TOGETHER

How long did it take you to get the feel of the game? Were there obstacles that kept hindering your progress? How did you finally overcome those obstacles?

Closer to God

Therefore, since we are surrounded by such a great cloud of
witnesses, let us throw off everything that hinders and the sin that
so easily entangles. And let us run with perseverance the race
marked out for us.

HEBREWS 12:1

Did you know that people who ran races in ancient times took off
almost all their clothes? That's because their clothing was made
of wool and was heavy, which would keep them from running
fast. The Bible says that's what sin does to us as we run the race
of life. Sin hinders and entangles us, preventing us from running
the best race we are capable of running.

Lord, help us cast off any sinful ways.

Remember Together

We have a choice to hold on to sin or to throw it off.

65

Ropes Course

$ $ $ / / / A A A # # Sp Su F

ACTIVITY

Many camps and colleges and universities have low ropes courses. These courses are a fantastic way to build trust among your kids. They are outstanding opportunities to grow their problem-solving skills and the ability to work with other people. So make a reservation at one of these institutions, pile in the car, and head out to the ropes course.

CLOSER TOGETHER

What did you think was the hardest task? What was the most fun? What did you learn about yourself? Your siblings?

Was not our father Abraham considered righteous for what he did when he offered his son Isaac on the altar? You see that his faith and his actions were working together, and his faith was made complete by what he did.

JAMES 2:21–22

God asked Abraham to prove his faith by sacrificing his only son, Isaac. Abraham took Isaac up on a mountain, tied him up, and was ready to kill him as a sacrifice to God, but God saw Abraham's faith and spared Isaac, instead providing a ram to be sacrificed. Faith is trusting God when it doesn't seem reasonable. We exercise faith by doing what God asks us to do.

God in heaven, may we have faith like Abraham and trust you completely.

REMEMBER TOGETHER

Faith in God and faith in others will help us accomplish much.

66

Readers Are Leaders

ACTIVITY

Pick a book to read together as a family. Christian classics like *The Pilgrim's Progress* or C. S. Lewis's books are a great place to start. Read a section every day, either during breakfast or after dinner, and talk about what the book is teaching you. When the book is completed, take each child out on an ice-cream date individually to hear what they thought of the book.

CLOSER TOGETHER

After each reading, ask questions like "What did this passage say to you?" On your ice-cream date, ask questions like "What was your favorite part?" and "How will this book help you in life?"

CLOSER TO GOD

"This is the covenant I will make with the people of Israel after that time," declares the LORD. "I will put my law in their minds and write it on their hearts. I will be their God, and they will be my people."

JEREMIAH 31:33

You will become the books you read and the people you hang around. Those words are somewhat hard to believe, but they're true. The people you hang around will influence you for good or bad. And the books you read will leave an indelible mark on your heart. God uses books to write on our hearts if we choose what we read wisely.

God, write your words on our heart.

REMEMBER TOGETHER

Books will change our lives.

Cornhole

Ⓢ Ⓢ ⋰ ⋰ Ⓐ Ⓐ # #

ACTIVITY

Find and download plans from the internet to construct your own cornhole game. If you are not very good at building things, then you can buy one at a local sporting goods store. Part of the fun of this activity is building and customizing your cornhole game by painting it with your favorite sports team's colors or a fun picture. When it's constructed and the paint has dried, have a cornhole tournament. Be sure to pick fair teams so everyone has fun!

CLOSER TOGETHER

Can you believe you built that yourselves? What was your favorite part, building or painting? Did you think the plans you downloaded were simple or difficult? What do you think about the idea that God has a plan for your life?

CLOSER TO GOD

"For I know the plans I have for you," declares the LORD, "plans to prosper you and not to harm you, plans to give you hope and a future. Then you will call on me and come and pray to me, and I will listen to you. You will seek me and find me when you seek me with all your heart."

JEREMIAH 29:11–13

Today you downloaded plans and built a cornhole game. Clearly the first thing you needed to do was make a plan. Did you know God has a plan for you? Indeed! From before the time you were born, he had a plan and a life marked out for you. How do we find God's plan? Well you can't look it up on the internet. You find God's plan when you seek him with all your heart.

Dear God, we want to know the plan that you have for our lives.

REMEMBER TOGETHER

God's plans are found when we seek him with our heart.

ACTIVITY

Slime, made famous by Nickelodeon, is a messy but fun thing to play with. There are many different "recipes" on the internet. Pick one you feel comfortable making. Set up a table in the garage or outside. Get the ingredients and make your slime. Then have fun "sliming" each other. Make sure everyone gets equal amounts of slime, and Dad, be prepared to get slimed the most!

CLOSER TOGETHER

Today you had fun making slime. What is something you had to do that wasn't so fun? How did you get through it? Why do you think, in life, that we have to do hard things?

CLOSER TO GOD

So make yourself an ark of cypress wood; make rooms in it and
coat it with pitch inside and out. This is how you are to build it:
The ark is to be three hundred cubits long, fifty cubits wide and
thirty cubits high.

GENESIS 6:14–15

Though making and playing with slime is fun, there are going to
be times when we will all have to do something that may sound
less than fun. In fact, it may seem too big of a task to handle.
That is a thought that might have gone through Noah's mind
when God asked him to build the ark. The measurements were
huge—three hundred cubits long by fifty cubits wide by thirty
cubits high. That would have been bigger by far than anything
Noah had ever seen, but he was faithful, and God blessed Noah
and his family.

*God in heaven, please give us the strength to handle the tasks
you put in front of us.*

REMEMBER TOGETHER

Some tasks are fun, and some are hard. Embrace them both.

69

Kids' Choice

ACTIVITY

Dad, it's kids' choice day, and whatever activity they choose together, you all have to do it with a joyful heart. If you really want to be brave, spend the afternoon letting each child pick an activity, and then you all do it. Remember you have a choice to be joyful as you do these activities.

CLOSER TOGETHER

Why did you choose the activity you chose? Was there one that was more fun than you expected? Was there one for which you really had to work at "being joyful"?

CLOSER TO GOD

"If serving the LORD seems undesirable to you, then choose for yourselves this day whom you will serve, whether the gods your ancestors served beyond the Euphrates, or the gods of the Amorites, in whose land you are living. But as for me and my household, we will serve the LORD."

JOSHUA 24:15

Did you know that every time you say yes to something, you are also saying no to many other things? For example, if I say yes to watching one particular TV show, then I am saying no to many, many others. Life is full of choice, and that is good. However, Satan desires to put poor choices in front of you every day. As a result, it's up to you to choose to either serve Satan and his evil choices or serve the Lord. Be careful. Sometimes Satan will put a bad choice in front of you that doesn't seem that bad at first, but in the long run, it can have terrible consequences.

As for us, we will serve the Lord!

REMEMBER TOGETHER

For every yes, there is also a no.

70

Project Saturday

ACTIVITY

Dad, spend the week talking to your kids about a project you are going to work on for Saturday. Maybe it's repairing a deck or installing a basketball hoop. Talk to them about how much fun it's going to be to do the project together. Show them plans on the internet or any kits you bought for the project. *Never* call it work until you are done.

CLOSER TOGETHER

Did today feel like work, or was it fun? Often when you call something work, it can make you not want to do it. Why were you so excited about today's project? Do you think you can have that kind of excitement for all your tasks?

148

CLOSER TO GOD

Start children off on the way they should go, and even when they
are old they will not turn from it.

PROVERBS 22:6

A good work ethic is one of the best qualities we can develop.
When we show a good work ethic, we actually honor God. By
doing our best, we give our best to him. How do we learn a good
work ethic? By following the example of others. Remember,
oftentimes more is caught than taught. So show each other how
to work hard.

Father, when we work, may we do it for your glory.

REMEMBER TOGETHER

There is value in hard work.

71

Axe Throwing

Ⓢ Ⓢ Ⓢ ⫶ ⫶ Ⓐ Ⓐ Ⓐ # # # #

ACTIVITY

Axe throwing has become popular because of the televised tournaments one can watch. It's a growing sport and can be a lot of fun if you follow the rules and precautions. Most recreation centers do have a minimum age requirement for axe throwing, so check that out before you go. Rent an "arena" and enjoy different contests the establishment offers. Order some refreshments and sharpen your throwing skills.

CLOSER TOGETHER

Was it a little intimidating at first when you held the axe in your hand? Were you amazed at how sharp they keep the axes so they are sure to stick in the target? Do you know how they sharpen axes? How do you stay sharp?

Closer to God

As iron sharpens iron, so one person sharpens another.
PROVERBS 27:17

Do your friends make you a better person? According to the verse above, they can. That's why choosing the right friends is so important. They will either make you a better person or not. Similarly, they will either make you closer to God or not, and that's a big deal. So choose your friends wisely and watch your love of God grow.

Dear Jesus, may we pick friends that help us love you more.

Remember Together

The right friends make all the difference.

Monster Truck Rally

$ $ $)) A A # # #

ACTIVITY

Find out when a monster truck rally is coming to an arena near you. Be sure to take ear protection as those monster trucks are loud. Laugh at the funny paint jobs and names of the trucks and sit in amazement as you watch the feats they perform. Be sure to grab some snacks at the concession stand.

CLOSER TOGETHER

Can you believe how loud those trucks were? Would it have been painful if you didn't bring your ear protection? Imagine now if you were hearing God's thunderous voice calling you to go to heaven…what would that be like?

CLOSER TO GOD

For the Lord himself will come down from heaven, with a loud
command, with the voice of the archangel and with the trumpet
call of God, and the dead in Christ will rise first.

1 THESSALONIANS 4:16

Isn't it interesting that God spoke the universe into existence?
That's the power of his voice. All he had to do was speak and
everything that we see came into being. Everything, that is,
except humans like us. God formed man out of the dust of the
earth and woman out of the rib of a man. However, just like the
beginning was marked by the voice of God, so will be the end of
all things. So we should always be listening for his voice.

Dear God, may we always be listening for your voice in our lives.

REMEMBER TOGETHER

We should always be listening for God's voice.

73

Car Show

ACTIVITY

Every summer, car enthusiasts bring their classic cars out of storage and enter them in classic car shows. Find one near you and go for the afternoon. Some car shows have official judges, but others let the attendees choose their favorite cars. Often there will be categories like sports car, sedan, truck. Spend the afternoon looking at cars and talking to the owners about the cars. You will learn a lot and make some new friends as well.

CLOSER TOGETHER

Which was your favorite car? Why? Which owner did you find most interesting? Do you think you'd ever want to own a classic car?

CLOSER TO GOD

Some trust in chariots and some in horses, but we trust in the name of the LORD our God.

PSALM 20:7

So many of us seek security in one way or another. We think if we go to the right school or live in the right house or drive the right car, then all will be fine. Our verse today says otherwise. In Bible times, kings would build mighty chariots and raise strong horses to help them fight battles. They sought "security" in chariots and horses, but God tells us to find our security in the name of the Lord God.

Lord, as we walk through life, may we find our security in you.

REMEMBER TOGETHER

While cars are super cool, they will not give us the security we find in God.

74

Girl Dad

Ⓢ Ⓢ Ⓢ ⟋ Ⓐ # #

ACTIVITY

So this is for dads with girls…you know—girl dads! Make an appointment at a nail salon or day spa but don't tell the girls what you're going to do. Pile them in the car and drive around a bit to see if they can guess. Arrive at your destination, and let them know that, today, they get to be pampered like the little ladies they are becoming. As you go through the experience, be sure to let them know how much you like the nail polish they've chosen or how pretty their hair looks. On the ride home, tell your daughters why they are beautiful to you all the time.

CLOSER TOGETHER

Were you surprised your dad would take you to a nail salon or spa? How did you feel when you first sat down? How did you feel when it was all done?

CLOSER TO GOD

Before a young woman's turn came to go in to King Xerxes, she had to complete twelve months of beauty treatments prescribed for the women, six months with oil of myrrh and six with perfumes and cosmetics.

ESTHER 2:12

Esther had to prepare herself for twelve months before she could see the king. That's a long time and a lot of perfume. The good news is that because of Jesus and his death and resurrection, we don't have to wait or prepare to be with the King of the universe… God! That's right, God is ready to talk to you and listen to your prayers twenty-four hours a day, seven days a week. So, what would you like to say to God?

God in heaven, thank you for hearing our prayers.

REMEMBER TOGETHER

True beauty comes from knowing we are children of God.

75

Family Bucket List

ACTIVITY

Sit around the dinner table with some snacks and drinks. Dream about what you'd like to do as a family. In other words, create a bucket list. Some may want to go for a dune buggy ride or race go-carts. Others may want to visit the mountains or the ocean or to see a famous place like the Statue of Liberty. No idea is too far out, so write them all down. As you plan future vacations and family times together, see how many activities you can check off your family bucket list.

CLOSER TOGETHER

Other than your own ideas, which bucket list idea seemed most fun to you? Which would you like to do first? Do you like to dream about the future? Why or why not?

CLOSER TO GOD

God permitting, we will do so.

HEBREWS 6:3

As Christ followers, we are to always make decisions using the phrase "God permitting." If we truly place our lives in his hands, then we want his will for us each and every day. We don't want to get caught up in always asking "What's God's will for my life?" because he has given us the ability to choose. But we should always choose which way to go based on the idea that we are seeking God's perfect will.

God, may we take every step every day with you.

REMEMBER TOGETHER

God places dreams in our hearts to give us hope for the future.

Acknowledgments

Dad, thanks for being such a good role model.

Torrey and Grace, you've made being a dad so much fun!

About the Authors

Jay and Laura Laffoon are all about helping busy couples stay happily married for life. They founded Celebrate Ministries, Inc., in 1995 to fulfill their passion for helping couples with comedy-infused marriage events and resources. They celebrate their own marriage of more than thirty years and make their home in Michigan.